Wild Baby
Animals
By Deborah Lock

Penguin
Random
House

Series Editor Deborah Lock
US Senior Editor Shannon Beatty
Project Art Editor / Illustrator Charlotte Jennings
Art Director Martin Wilson
Senior Producer, Pre-production Nikoleta Parasaki

Reading Consultant Linda Gambrell, Ph.D

First American Edition, 2016
Published in the United States by DK Publishing
345 Hudson Street, New York, New York 10014

A catalog record for this book is available from the Library of Congress.
ISBN: 978-1-4654-4599-5 (Paperback)
ISBN: 978-1-4654-4598-8 (Hardcover)

Printed and bound in China
DK books are available at special discounts when purchased in bulk for sales promotions, premiums,
fund-raising, or educational use. For details, contact: DK Publishing Special Markets, 345 Hudson
Street, New York, New York 10014 or SpecialSales@dk.com.

The publisher would like to thank the following
for their kind permission to reproduce their photographs:
(Key: a-above; b-below/bottom; c-center; f-far; l-left; r-right; t-top)
1 FLPA: Suzi Eszterhas / Minden Pictures. **4 Getty Images:** Les Stocker / Oxford Scientific (c).
5 Getty Images: Les Stocker / Oxford Scientific (tc). **7 Alamy Images:** Dmitriy Shironosov (b). **Getty Images:**
Danielle Kiemel / Moment Open (cra). **8 Corbis:** Mitsuaki Iwago / Minden Pictures (c). **9 Alamy Images:** Huetter,
C. / Arco Images GmbH (cr). **Getty Images:** Mint Images - Frans Lanting (tl). **10 FLPA:** Anup Shah / Minden
Pictures. **11 Alamy Images:** Louise Heusinkveld (tl). **FLPA:** Anup Shah / Minden Pictures (cr, bl). **12 FLPA:** Ingo
Arndt / Minden Pictures (cr); Gerry Ellis / Minden Pictures (tr); Michael Durham (fclb). **13 FLPA:** Michael
Durham (tr); Frans Lanting (cra); Michael Durham / Minden Pictures (fcr); Suzi Eszterhas / Minden Pictures (clb);
John Zimmermann (bl). Fotolia: Tujian (cr). **15 Getty Images:** Sven-Erik Arndt / Picture Press (cr); Tier Und
Naturfotografie J und C Sohns / Photographer's Choice (bl). **17 naturepl.com:** ARCO (tr). **18 Alamy Images:** Life
on white (b). **Getty Images:** Gerard Lacz / Visuals Unlimited (t). **19 Dreamstime.com:** Aspenphoto (cr). **naturepl.
com:** Thomas Lazar (t). **20-21 Alamy Images:** Nano Calvo / VWPICS / Visual&Written SL. **21 Getty Images:**
Science Faction / Steven Kazlowski (t). **22 Getty Images:** Tom Brakefield / Digital Vision (cla); Mint Images - Frans
Lanting (cb). **23 Alamy Images:** Edo Schmidt (cb). **Getty Images:** T. Davis / W. Bilenduke / Iconica (t). **24 Alamy
Images:** Mark J. Barrett. **25 FLPA:** Lydie Gigerichova / Imagebroker. **26 Dreamstime.com:** Ponsuwan. **27 FLPA:**
Imagebroker,Thomas Dressler / Imagebroker (c); Terry Whittaker (tl). **28 Alamy Images:** Yvette Cardozo. **29
Alamy Images:** Malcolm Schuyl (crb). **Dreamstime.com:** Paul Banton (cla). **30 Getty Images:** Altrendo Nature
(l). **31 Dreamstime.com:** Isselee (bl). **32-33 FLPA:** Bernd Zoller / Imagebroker. **34 Alamy Images:** Juanma
Aparicio. **35 Dreamstime.com:** Lidian Neeleman / Caramaria (tr). **FLPA:** Jurgen & Christine Sohns (cl). **36
FLPA:** Suzi Eszterhas / Minden Pictures (t). **37 Dreamstime.com:** Anankkml. **38 Alamy Images:** Stephen Meese
(tl). **Fotolia:** Eric Isselee (br). **39 FLPA:** Thomas Marent / Minden Pictures. **40 Dorling Kindersley:** Jerry Young.
41 Dreamstime.com: Rudy Umans / Rudyumans. **42 FLPA:** Shin Yoshino / Minden Pictures (br).
Endpapers: **Alamy Images:** Life on white. **Jacket images:** *Front:* **Corbis:** PunchStock: DLILLC (c).
Fotolia: Eric Isselee (ca) (cra) (bl). **Getty Images:** Martin Harvey / Lifesize (cla);
Back: **FLPA:** Michael Durham / Minden Pictures bl

All other images © Dorling Kindersley Limited
For further information see: www.dkimages.com

A WORLD OF IDEAS:
SEE ALL THERE IS TO KNOW
www.dk.com

Contents

Chapter 1 Birth

Baby squirrels are born in a warm and cozy nest.

ZZZ!

They have no fur and their eyes are closed.

They start to climb
at eight weeks old.

Roly-poly!

Rabbit kits are born deep inside **burrows**.

They drink their mom's milk for the first few weeks.

6

By one month
old, they spend
most of their
time outside.

Wriggle!

At birth, a kangaroo joey is the size of a jelly bean.

The joey crawls up its mom's fur and falls into her pouch.

The joey spends
more than
six months
in the pouch.

9

Cuddle!

A gray langur monkey's baby has bright orange fur.

It spends all day in the trees.

It takes about
three months
for its fur
to change color.

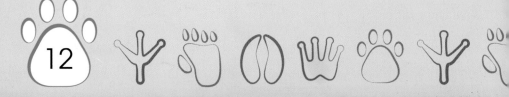

Birth Stories

Birds lay eggs.
Their babies **hatch**
out of shells.

Amphibians lay
thousands of eggs.
Their babies spend
the first part of
their lives in water.

Fish also lay eggs.
Some lay millions
of eggs.

Most **reptiles** lay eggs.
Their babies also grow
inside eggs.

Most **mammals**
give birth
to live babies.

Chapter 2 Explore

Blink!

Bear cubs are born

in twos or

threes.

A bear gives birth in
a **den** in midwinter.

In spring,
the cubs
peek out
for the
first time.

They play and learn
how to find food.

sn**iff!**

Furry fox
cubs are
wide-eyed
and hear
very well.

There are many sights
and sounds for them
to explore.

They jump around
and practice their
pouncing skills.

Skip!

A fawn runs and leaps
around on long, nimble legs.

But when it
senses danger,

18

it curls up
and hides
in leaves.

Its **speckled** pattern makes
the fawn hard to see.

19

Splash!

An otter pup
needs to be
able to swim
and dive.

20

But at first, a sea otter
pup can only float.

It has to shed
its newborn fur
and then it can
go under the water.

Body Warmers

Ice is nice when you have a warm fur coat.

Keep warm together in a huddle.

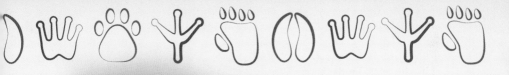

Snuggle against mom in a snowy world.

All wrapped up by mom's long tail.

Chapter 3 Play

Stretch!

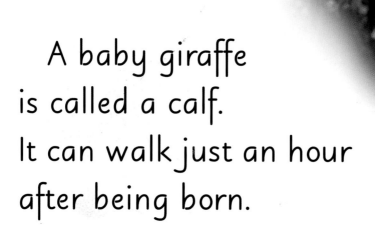

A baby giraffe
is called a calf.
It can walk just an hour
after being born.

It quickly
learns to use
its long neck
to reach up
high to **nibble**
leaves.

It spends
as much as
18 hours
a day eating.

Spray!

An elephant calf
sucks its trunk
like a human baby
sucks its thumb.

The calf then
learns to use
its trunk to
wash and drink.

It finds out its trunk can
pull up plants and be used
for lots of other tasks.

scratch!

Cheetah cubs leave
the den at about
eight weeks old.

The cubs play together to learn to be good hunters.

They stalk, chase, pounce, and wrestle.

Flash!

Ostrich chicks
have long legs
and two toes
on each foot.

At one month old,
they can run very fast.

They grow fast, too.
They are as tall as
their mom at
six months old.

Family Fun

Some baby animals, like lion cubs, grow up in large family groups.

A pride is a family of lions.

Lionesses care for each others' cubs.

Cubs play with Dad.

Cubs learn together.

Chapter 4 Learn

Munch!

Baby gorillas stay with
their moms for three years.

They learn
to pick fruit
and leaves,

and munch on
stalks and roots.

They also learn
to build nests
out of plants.

Creep!

Tiger cubs stay with their moms for nearly two years.

They learn how to **crouch** down low, and slowly creep forward.

They learn when to pounce
and catch their dinner.

It takes time to learn
how to hunt on their own.

Yawn!

Baby orangutans hang around with their moms for seven years.

They have a lot to learn about living in the jungle.

They swing around, find food, make nests in trees, and use leaves as umbrellas.

snap!

Crocodilian babies learn
to hunt very quickly.

They are born knowing
how to swim and how
to catch small animals.

40

But they
have to practice
to get better at
hunting the bigger animals.

Weird or Cute?

How would you describe these babies?

European owl

Leopard gecko

Red panda

Wild Baby Animals Quiz

1. What is a baby kangaroo called?
2. What does a fawn do when it senses danger?
3. How do baby penguins keep warm?
4. What is a group of lions called?
5. How long does a baby orangutan stay with its mom?

Answers on page 45.

Glossary

amphibian animal that lives in water and on land

burrow hole that leads to underground home with tunnels

crouch bend low

den animal's hidden home

hatch break out of a shell

mammals group of animals, including humans, that have fur or hair, are warm-blooded, and have backbones

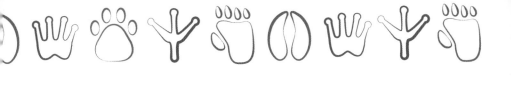

nibble take small bites of food

pounce sudden jump or swoop onto something

reptile animal with dry, scaly skin that lives on land

speckled covered with small spots of color

Answers to the Wild Baby Animals Quiz:
1. Joey; 2. Curls up and hides in the leaves; 3. They huddle together;
4. Pride; 5. Seven years.

Guide for Parents

DK Readers is a four-level interactive reading adventure series for children, developing the habit of reading widely for both pleasure and information. These books have an exciting main narrative interspersed with a range of reading genres to suit your child's reading ability. Each book is designed to develop your child's reading skills, fluency, grammar awareness, and comprehension in order to build confidence and engagement when reading.

Ready for a *Beginning to Read* book

YOUR CHILD SHOULD

- be familiar with using beginning letter sounds and context clues to figure out unfamiliar words.
- be aware of the need for a slight pause at commas and a longer one at periods.
- alter his/her expression for questions and exclamations.

A VALUABLE AND SHARED READING EXPERIENCE

For many children, reading requires much effort, but adult participation can make this both fun and easier. So here are a few tips on how to use this book with your child.

TIP 1 Check out the contents together before your child begins:

- read the text about the book on the back cover.
- flip through the book and stop to chat about the contents page together to heighten your child's interest and expectation.
- make use of unfamiliar or difficult words on the page in a brief discussion.
- chat about the nonfiction reading features used in the book, such as headings, captions, recipes, lists, or charts.

TIP 2 Support your child as he/she reads the story pages:

- give the book to your child to read and turn the pages.
- where necessary, encourage your child to break a word into syllables, sound out each one, and then flow the syllables together. Ask him/her to reread the sentence to check the meaning.
- when there's a question mark or an exclamation point, encourage your child to vary his/her voice as he/she reads the sentence. Demonstrate how to do this if it is helpful.

TIP 3 Chat at the end of each page:

- the factual pages tend to be more difficult than the story pages, and are designed to be shared with your child.
- ask questions about the text and the meaning of the words used. These help to develop comprehension skills and awareness of the language used.

A FEW ADDITIONAL TIPS

- Always encourage your child to try reading difficult words by themselves. Praise any self-corrections, for example, "I like the way you sounded out that word and then changed the way you said it, to make sense."
- Try to read together everyday. Reading little and often is best. These books are divided into manageable chapters for one reading session. However, after 10 minutes, only keep going if your child wants to read on.
- Read other books of different types to your child just for enjoyment and information.

Series consultant, **Dr. Linda Gambrell**, Distinguished Professor of Education at Clemson University, has served as President of the National Reading Conference, the College Reading Association, and the International Reading Association.

Index